Write Your Book on the Side

How to Write and Publish Your First Nonfiction Kindle Book While Working a Full-Time Job

(Even if You Don't Have a Lot of Time and Don't Know Where to Start)

By

Hassan Osman

Write Your Book on the Side: How to Write and Publish Your First Nonfiction Kindle Book While Working a Full-Time Job (Even if You Don't Have a Lot of Time and Don't Know Where to Start)

Table of Contents

Is This Book for You?

Thanks for picking up a copy of this book.

Let's start with a quick check on whether you're in the right place.

This book is for you if:

- You're working a full-time job.
- You're interested in writing a nonfiction book.
- You don't know where to start.
- You have little time to spend on writing.
- You don't know much about the publishing process.

It's a short, straightforward book that will give you everything you need to write your first nonfiction Kindle book and become a published author. No fluff. No hidden secrets. No false promises. Just an easy plan that works.

Now let's cover whom this is *not* for.

This book is not for you if:

- You're interested in writing a fiction book. (I have no experience in that field.)
- You've published a book before. (This book is for first-time authors.)
- You want to publish an ebook on your own blog or on a platform other than Amazon Kindle. (I focus exclusively on the Amazon Kindle Direct Publishing (KDP) platform, and explain why it's the best option for your first book.)
- You've already read a ton of other books and blog posts about how to write and publish a Kindle book. (I

doubt you'll learn something new.)

With that said, if you're in the right place, continue reading!

Introduction

I don't have time to write books.

I work a demanding full-time job that keeps me quite busy.[1]

I'm also married with two little kids.

Between work and life, my schedule gets pretty crazy. Family comes first to me, and I never sacrifice spending quality time with my wife and daughters at the expense of work. So this makes it even more challenging to find the time to write a book.

To make things worse, I'm a slow writer. It physically pains me to write, and I can barely go through a couple of lines at a time before coming up with excuses to do something else, like checking Facebook.

Plus, I'm someone who's generally lazy. I would rather watch another rerun of *Band of Brothers* than sit down to type at my keyboard.

Yet with all those challenges, I managed to publish not just one but two Amazon Kindle books, both of which hit the #1 Amazon Bestseller list in their categories.

The book you're reading now is the third. And I've already started working on the fourth and the fifth.

If I can do it—someone who holds a full time job, and is

---

[1] I'm a full-time employee at Cisco Systems, where I work as a (very busy) PMO Manager. Views are my own and not those of Cisco.

a full time father and procrastinator—then so can you. I guarantee it.

Why I wrote this book (and why you should read it)

There are many books about how to write a book.

So many, in fact, that I almost didn't write this one.

I felt that everything I wanted to say had already been covered several times over and from multiple angles.

However, I decided to write it because of one simple reason:

There is no other book like it.

I don't mean that in a self-aggrandizing, "it's the one and only" sense. In fact, there's nothing earth-shattering or entirely original about this book at all.

What I mean is that there isn't a single resource that concisely covers the questions that busy people frequently have, such as:

"How do I find the time to write?"

"Where do I start?"

"How do I pick a topic that people will be interested in?"

"What's the best way to get the book published?"

"How many words in length should the book be?"

"How much money can I really make from a book?"

And on and on...

The answers to those questions are all out there, but the information is dispersed in multiple books, articles, and videos.

The problem is that working people are already too busy to write books, which means that they don't have the time to sift through a ton of resources to figure things out.

I know this first-hand because I've been there. I've struggled to find a short, well-written book that addresses all the challenges that I had when I first started years ago.

To this day, I still cannot find a helpful "one-stop-shop" guide that covers what part-time authors need to know in a quick and digestible way.

So I wrote this one.

It's a concise book that'll give you a step-by-step process to write and publish your book on the side.

Here are a couple of reasons why you should read it.

Reason 1: It focuses on the stuff that matters

There are two problems with all the information about book publishing.

First, there's too much of it.

You can easily get overwhelmed by the sheer amount of information available to you. Every aspect of writing and publishing a book has an entire ecosystem dedicated to it. I did a quick online search and found 18 different books about "Avoiding writer's block," and 48,800 articles about "How to write a book description."

Who has the time to go through all of that?

The second problem is that there's a lot of *conflicting* information.

Every expert has a different opinion about what works and what doesn't, and that makes the first problem even worse. Not only do you have to worry about sifting through a boatload of resources, but you also have to agonize about which decision to make.

So you get paralyzed and you give up on writing.

The good news is that I've done all that research for you.

I've followed nearly every major authority figure in this space: Pat Flynn, James Altucher, Steve Scott, Tim Ferriss, and many, many more.

I've studied their books, listened to their podcasts, watched their videos, and read their blog posts.

I've tested what works and what doesn't, and summarized all of that for you in this book.

The biggest advantage is that I focus only on the important stuff you need to know to write and publish your book in the shortest time possible.

I'll tell you what tasks are considered "must haves" (the steps that you shouldn't skip) and what tasks are "nice to haves" (the steps that are optional, but could be advantageous).

I'll also explain what you should spend money on and what you should probably do on your own. All of that in a simple, easy-to-follow plan.

Reason 2: It's realistic and transparent

The second reason why you should read this book is that you won't find any hyper-inflated assertions or crazy numbers here.

Claims such as "Write your book in 24 hours" or "Make $40,000 a month with Kindle books" might be possible for someone who's already published a library full of books, or for someone who's extremely talented or lucky. However, they're certainly not probable for the average author, and particularly not a first-time one.

I've read a lot of those click-bait resources myself.

A few actually contain some helpful tips, but for the most part they're total hogwash.

When I wrote this book, I thought of my close family and friends as my primary audience, so I'm 100% honest and transparent about everything I cover.

I share realistic numbers about how much money I make, and how much time it takes to finish a book. I also explain why hitting the Amazon bestselling list isn't so much of a big deal and how it's relatively easy to get on it.

The Only Thing That Matters (and Rule #1)

There is one—and *only* one—thing that matters about your book:

Your reader.

In other words, your customer.

It's the person who buys your book with the expectation that they will get more value from it than the amount they paid for it in cash and time.[2]

Everything else is secondary.

Forget the testimonials. Forget the sales. Forget the money and the reviews. Forget the cover design.

Ignore all that noise because it doesn't matter as much as your customer.

If you focus primarily on writing your book with your reader in mind, then you are going to be successful as an author.

Which brings us to Rule #1, defined as follows:

Rule #1: Write a really, really useful book.

---

[2] This is from a blog post I wrote once entitled *"The Science of Getting Rich in 15 Words (aka The 15 Word Rule)"* which is based on the book by Wallace Wattles. You can read the post here: http://www.parttimewebpreneur.com/the-science-of-getting-rich-in-15-words/

That's it.

A simple but very profound rule which should be your North Star throughout the entire book-writing process.

It's a rule that keeps your attention focused solely on your reader.

You might ask, *"What does 'useful' really mean?"*

Here are three explanations:

1) Useful means helpful

When someone buys a nonfiction book, they're typically looking to solve a specific problem or to address a pain point that they have. So give them a helpful book that solves their issue by challenging yourself with the following question: *"How will my reader's life improve after they read my book?"*

2) Useful means short

Your book should be short and concise. Many people have this misconception that a publication has to be the size of an aircraft manual to qualify as a legitimate book. But that's not true. Most readers don't have a lot of time to go through an endless manuscript. They want to get to a solution as fast as possible, and without having to sift through a mountain of fluff. So focus on making your book long enough to get the point across. No more, no less.

3) Useful means well written

Finally, your book should be well written. This doesn't mean that your book needs to be worthy of a Pulitzer Prize. It just means that you give it your own personal best. Of course, the book should flow properly in terms of content and be free of mistakes in spelling and grammar. But you should also go above and beyond to make your book a great experience for your readers, and not just slap something together for the sake of being able to say you've written a book.

The bottom line about Rule #1 is this: your readers should be happy that they spent their money and their valuable time on reading your book. So make it helpful, make it short, and write it well.

All About the Money

Let's get into how much money you can make from a Kindle book.

I wanted to address this topic early on because there's a lot of curiosity and misinformation about it.

Many people ask me how much money they can make, and I always give them the same answer:

I don't know. No one does.

It could be as low as *$2 a month*, or as high as *$3,000 a day*. It depends on the topic, the market, and so many other factors that it's hard to say. Even successful authors who have hit it big with one book admit that they couldn't figure out a repeatable formula for their subsequent ones.

However, I can tell you how much money I personally make.

Before I share my numbers though, let me give you a little background.

I have published two Amazon Kindle books.

The first is called *Influencing Virtual Teams*, which is about managing remote employees, and the second is called *Don't Reply All*, which is about communicating effectively through email.

Both those books cover niche topics. They target managers in corporations who want to get better at managing and communicating with their team members. Neither book was designed for a mass audience.

I mention that because I want to put things in perspective for you. If my books appealed to a bigger market, such as those who are interested in cooking or exercising, then I might make more sales simply because there are more potential customers.

So the numbers might be a bit different in your case.

How much money I make

I sell between one and five Kindle versions of each book per day. The Kindle version of each book is priced at $2.99, and I make a 70 percent royalty from every sale (Amazon's cut is 30 percent). So that means I make $2.09 in profit per book.

If you do the math, that translates to around $60 to $300 in profit per month, per book. My average hovers around $200 per month.

That's not a very high number, but it's also not a low number. I always say $200 is greater than $0. It's a nice check that pays for a couple of bills here and there.

Keep in mind however, that those figures are mostly organic sales through Amazon's traffic. So the $200 per month figure is during my steady-state phase when there are no special events or marketing efforts going on.

However, when I do get media mentions, such as when someone hosts me on their podcast or blog, then I get a nice bump in sales for that month. For example, my income rose to around $600 in a recent month because my book was featured in a couple of articles. So it fluctuates.

Three things to keep in mind about the money

Here are three things you should keep in mind about the money you can make.

1) Legacy > Currency

The first is that *legacy* is more important than *currency*. I heard this phrase once from Gary Vaynerchuk and it stuck with me since.

There is no shame in wanting to make money. We all like having more of it to live a better life. However, by prioritizing the money over creating quality, you'll lose in the long run.

Writing a nonfiction book should primarily be about establishing credibility and authority in a specific domain. Your aim should be to become a published author and respected thought leader in your market. So focus on a "legacy-first" mindset over a "money-first" one, and the money will come later.

2) It's passive income

The second thing about the money is that it's passive income that doesn't require your involvement in the sales process. Amazon does everything for you. It hosts your book and distributes it to your readers. It handles payments, returns, and customer service. It even markets your book for you (to a certain extent). All you do is sit back and collect the check at the end of the month.

The biggest benefit is that your book will become part of an infrastructure that is ready for a sales spike due to an event months or even years after you publish. It becomes part of a system that requires the same amount of your "effort" to sell one book as it does to sell a million. So if you get lucky and someone famous mentions your book six months after you publish, you'll get a huge surge of sales that won't require any additional labor on your part.

3) More money "because of" than "from"

The third thing is that you'll probably make more money *because of* your book than *from* your book. That's because your book will offer you opportunities to upsell more expensive products or services down the line.

Publishing a nonfiction book is like having a resume on steroids. It opens up many doors for you that you don't expect.

For example, it could help you get more exposure through speaking engagements or consulting gigs. It could also support you in getting a better job or even a promotion in your current one.

All those opportunities have a much higher monetary value associated with them than direct book sales.

So the return on investment of writing a book is 100% worth it.

Simply focus on Rule #1 (write a really, really useful

book) and worry about everything later.

Why You Should Publish on Amazon KDP

If you're already convinced that self-publishing an ebook on Amazon is the best route for you as a first-time author, then you might want to skip this chapter.

But if you have doubts, or want to verify that this is indeed the best approach, then read on.

Quick overview

Amazon's ebook publishing division is called Kindle Direct Publishing (KDP). It's a platform that allows authors to publish their books in less than 20 minutes and have them ready to be sold worldwide within 48 hours.

There are many other publishing options besides Amazon KDP, and I've tried a few myself.

However, KDP is hands-down the best place for you to get the best return on your book, especially for a first-time author.

Let me walk you through a step-by-step decision process that explains why.

Traditional publishing or self-publishing?

The first major decision you need to make is whether you should go with traditional publishing or self-publishing.

Traditional publishing is the old-school method of

publishing books. It involves working with a literary agent and submitting your book to a publishing house. It's a very long and tedious process. Once you sign their contract, the publisher also has full control over everything, including the title, cover design, and marketing strategy. So you have very little say in the whole process. While there are some advantages with traditional publishing, such as having a professional team to work with and getting better distribution in bookstores, for most first-time authors of nonfiction books the cons outweigh the pros.

On the other hand, self-publishing is basically doing everything yourself. You're responsible for the topic, structure, content, design, and marketing. This is a good and a bad thing. Good because it's your book and your rules. Bad because you have to carry the entire weight alone. You have to find and hire the right people to help out with things like editing your manuscript and designing your cover. This adds a little bit more management overhead time.

Another important point to consider is that if you self-publish, you keep 100 percent ownership of your book. If you want to revise your book, or put on a new cover, you can do that because you own your book. No one else has any contractual claim to any part of it.

So when you consider all the angles, self-publishing is a much better and faster route to go with than traditional publishing.

Decision: Self-publish.

Sell independently or on a marketplace?

After deciding on the self-publishing track, the next

decision is whether you should sell independently or sell on an established marketplace.

Selling independently means selling your book on your own blog or website where you self-host everything. You'll need to set up a payment processor to receive payments (such as PayPal), and install some form of shopping cart software to distribute the book (such as E-junkie). You will also have to deal with minor details such as the design of the sales page and even the color of the buy button.

So you have total control, but it'll take up a bit of your time. The main advantage of this is that you can offer higher price points through packaged deals. For example, you can sell your book with some audio files and a private coaching session for $147. However, the disadvantage is that you'll need a huge following and a comprehensive marketing strategy to be successful. And if you're not a well-known author, getting a lot of traffic to your site to convert is going to be a challenge. Moreover, you'll need to spend a ton of time on things like technical issues and on customer service, which are headaches you want to avoid.

On the other side of the spectrum, a marketplace is platform that sells multiple books published by many authors. It's an established site that handles everything from payment systems to downloads to customer returns. All you do as an author is upload the book to the marketplace, and it takes care of everything for you. You just get charged a fee on every sale. Amazon is one such marketplace, but there are also many others like Apple iBooks, Barnes & Noble Nook, and Sony Kobo.

The advantage of marketplaces is that people visit them with an intent to buy. So you already have high-quality traffic visiting your book's page without spending a lot of effort to drive it. And those prospective customers usually have their credit card numbers saved for quick and easy purchasing.

So the marketplace wins here because the advantage of having millions of customers ready to spend their money on a marketplace outweighs the potential profit of selling independently.

Decision: Sell on a marketplace.

All marketplaces or just Amazon?

After deciding on a marketplace, the next question is whether you should list your book on all marketplaces or only on Amazon.

If you list your book on all marketplaces (i.e., Amazon *and* iBooks, Kobo, Nook, Smashwords, etc.), you'll naturally get more exposure for your book. The more platforms you publish your book on, the bigger the audience that will see it, which theoretically means more sales.

However, the disadvantage is that you will have to format the book according to each one of these platform's requirements, which could be a hassle. Moreover, you lose one big advantage: getting an Amazon exclusive deal.

An Amazon exclusive deal means that you choose to publish *only* on Amazon's KDP platform by enrolling in a program called Amazon KDP Select.

KDP Select offers authors higher ebook royalties in some international countries, better promotional deals (like giving your ebook away for free for a few days during every 90-day period), and greater exposure in the Kindle Unlimited and Kindle Owners' Lending Library programs (where Amazon members can borrow your ebook).

Publishing exclusively with Amazon, however, means that you're not allowed to publish anywhere else. No Apple iBooks. No Nook. No personal site. Not even as a free giveaway on your blog. So you'll be giving up on all of the other platforms for this exclusive deal.

This is obviously a sacrifice.

For me however, enrolling in KDP Select makes a lot of sense.

Here are three reasons why.

Reason #1: It's Amazon

To this day, Amazon is by far the number one company in terms of ebook sales. It dominates 85% of the ebook market and has the widest audience. So you'll be partnering with the biggest platform in the world to sell your book. You can't go wrong with that.

Reason #2: Anyone can read the ebook

Readers on the other platforms can still read your ebook. That's because publishing on KDP does not mean that readers only with a Kindle *device* can read the book (a common misconception). Readers who have an iPhone, an iPad, an Android phone, or even just a laptop can still read your book by downloading the free Kindle App on those devices. So anyone can read your Kindle ebook even if you publish exclusively on Amazon.

Reason #3: It's only for 90 days

Amazon's enrollment in KDP Select is only for 90 days at a time. So you're not bound for life. After 90 days, you can break the exclusive agreement and sell your book on all the other marketplaces.

I know it sounds a bit illogical to go with just one marketplace instead of all of them, but the lion's share of sales will come from Amazon anyway, and KDP Select will give you a huge leg up on that.

Decision: Amazon Exclusive (through KDP Select).

Multiple formats or ebook only?

After deciding on an Amazon exclusive deal through KDP Select, the final decision is whether you should publish your book in an ebook-only format, or in all formats (i.e., ebook, paperback, and audiobook).

My recommendation is focus on the ebook version only when you first publish because the other formats will require a lot of time on your end in terms of prepping and formatting.

Side note: I use the words "ebook" and "book" interchangeably. The line between the two is blurry anyway because it's relatively simple to create a physical book from an ebook version through a technology called print-on-demand. More about that later.

In addition, ebook sales now surpass print and audio sales by far, so you would be starting with the format that sells the most anyway.

Decision: Ebook only, at least initially.

In summary, the easiest, fastest, most profitable, and least time-consuming route to publish your book on the side is to self-publish an ebook exclusively on Amazon's Kindle Direct Publishing platform through KDP Select.

That's it.

Still having doubts?

If you still have any doubts about the decision points above, don't stress too much. That's because after you publish your ebook you can still change your mind about every decision.

For example, after you launch your ebook you can create a paperback and audiobook.

You can also break your KDP select contract after 90 days and sell your book on other marketplaces.

You can then choose to sell it on your own blog as part of a packaged deal, or give it away for free as a marketing tool.

That's exactly what I did with my *Influencing Virtual Teams* book. I published it as an ebook-only version when I first launched it. Then, after a full year or so, I created the print and audiobook versions. I then broke my KDP Select contract and gave away my book for free as part of special promotions.

If I wanted to, I could have also published traditionally by signing a deal with a publisher.

So don't worry so much about starting with Amazon KDP Select. Every decision is reversible.

Your Free Gift

As a thank-you for your purchase, I'm offering a couple of files as a free bonus:

1) One-page book summary: A downloadable one-page PDF file that summarizes all the contents of this book for you on a single page. You can save it on your desktop or print it out as a handy reminder of all the steps you'll take when writing your first book.

2) Free copy of my bestselling book ($9.99 value): A downloadable PDF copy of my #1 Amazon bestselling book *Influencing Virtual Teams*. Even if you're not interested in the topic of virtual teams, you can quickly skim through it to come up with ideas for your own book. Think of it as a template that'll help you with things like formatting, content creation, font styles, layout, and word choice. It's the perfect example of what your book might look like after you follow the steps in this book.

Visit the following page to download your free bonus:

http://www.thecouchmanager.com/wbsbonus

The Process at a Glance

Here's the entire end-to-end process of writing and publishing your book on the side:

- Step 1: Choose a General Topic
- Step 2: Narrow It Down
- Step 3: Choose a Title and Subtitle
- Step 4: Test and Iterate
- Step 5: Outline Your Book
- Step 6: Write Your Book
- Step 7: Edit Your Book
- Step 8: Format Your Book
- Step 9: Design a Cover
- Step 10: Publish Your Book
- Step 11 [Optional]: Launch Your Book
- Step 12 [Optional]: Turn Your Book into an Amazon #1 Best Seller
- Step 13 [Optional]: Gather Emails from Readers
- Step 14 [Optional]: Expand Into Other Formats

Note that steps 1 through 10 are mandatory. Those are the "must have" steps that you should follow to make your book a success.

The remaining steps (11 through 14) are marked as optional. Those are the ones that are "nice to haves." So they're not really necessary to publish your book, but they'll give you a nice advantage if you have the time and energy to do them.

In the next few chapters, I'll get into the details about what each step includes.

Your Top FAQs Answered

Let's begin with a few answers to the top frequently asked questions (FAQs) and concerns many people have.

I'll expand a bit more on all those answers throughout the book, but I wanted to address them at a high-level early on.

How can I find the time to write a book on the side?
You force yourself to. There is no other way. You sit down for 30 minutes a day, five days a week, and just write. It doesn't matter if what you write doesn't make sense. You'll revise it all later anyway. The secret is momentum. By forcing yourself to write, you'll get all your thoughts out on paper, which is the hardest part.

I don't have 30 minutes a day.
Of course you do. Wake up 30 minutes early, or go to bed 30 minutes late. Or skip your favorite reality TV show. Anyone can find 30 minutes a day if they put their mind to it.

How long will it take me to finish a book at that rate?
Six months, give or take. It will depend on your writing speed, your book length, and what you're going to outsource.

Do I need any special tools or apps to write or publish?
No. Microsoft Word (or something similar) is all you need.

What if I can't write?
You can hire someone to write the book for you (i.e., a ghostwriter). Many business leaders and politicians use ghostwriters for their books, and there's nothing wrong with that approach. However, keep in mind that even with ghostwriting, you'll still have to do quite a bit of writing yourself (outlining, giving feedback, editing, etc.) and that the book might not end up feeling like it's yours. It might also get pretty expensive if you want to find a ghostwriter who does high quality work.

How do I self-publish my book on Amazon KDP?
The process is very simple. You only need two things. The first is your finished book in a properly formatted Microsoft Word file. (The directions for formatting are published on the Amazon KDP site. They're easy to follow.) The second is 20 minutes of your time to upload it on Amazon's Kindle Direct Publishing platform, where you select things like your book's price, categories, and keywords. Your book will then appear within 48 hours in the Amazon marketplace for people to buy it.

How long should an ebook be?
Around 10,000 to 12,000 words. Amazon uses a word count instead of a page count because the number of pages depends on the screen size. That range translates to approximately 60 to 70 pages of a standard size book. For reference, one of my books is 10,230 words, and the other is 12,583 words in length.

Do I need to spend any money on the process?
No. You can do it all yourself, for free. But I do
recommend that you spend money on things like cover
design, professional editing, and formatting. We'll
discuss why and how much you can expect to spend
later.

Step 1: Choose a General Topic

When you've decided to write a book on the side, the first step is to choose a topic.

The goal here is to pick a subject that satisfies two conditions: people want to read about it and you want to write about it.

While this might sound elementary, a lot of first-time authors don't put much thought into this step. They immediately jump into picking a title and start writing their book. But this step is important because it's the foundation for everything else.

Even if you already have a general topic in mind, make sure it fits into this framework before you move forward.

Four circles

The best way to explain how to choose a topic is to think of a Venn diagram with four circles that intersect in the middle.

Three of those circles are mandatory, and one of them is optional.

Circle 1 is labeled "Interest," Circle 2 is "Experience," and Circle 3 is "Market." Circle 4, which is optional, is "Job-Related."

The objective is to jot down ideas in each of those circles and to pick the ones that show up at the intersection.

You've probably seen some version of this exercise

before. That's because most successful authors advocate following a similar process when choosing a topic for their own books. So it works.

Here's what each circle is about.

Circle 1: Interest

The first circle is about ideas that you're interested in. Interest doesn't mean being madly in love with the subject of your book. It just means that it excites you on some level. If your book becomes a hit, chances are you'll be doing a lot more writing and talking about the topic on news sites, blogs, or podcasts. So if you're not very interested in the topic now, you're not going to be interested in it later.

When you're thinking about ideas for this circle, consider what you enjoy doing or reading when you're not forced to. List your hobbies and pastimes, which are great indicators of what you're naturally interested in.

Circle 2: Experience

The second circle is about areas in which you have some experience. Don't confuse *experience* with being an *expert.*

Experience only means that you know a little bit more about a topic than what the average person does. If you've had a unique personal experience that you think is worth sharing with your readers, then that would qualify as an idea for this circle. Jot down ideas by thinking through your employment history and academic courses you've taken in the past. The main takeaway here is to list things you actually know something about, because it will show if you don't.

Circle 3: Market

The third circle is about ideas that have an existing market. An existing market means that people are actively purchasing products about the area you're writing about. This could include information, services, products, or other books. The point is to make sure there's a *need* that people are actually paying money for.

This is important because a non-existent market means that you won't have enough customers or readers for your book. It's not very wise to write a book about something like *The History of Hairspray in Angola* if no one wants to buy it.

Researching for an existing market can be the subject of an entire three-hour course, but for your first book, you don't really need to go through all of that. A shortcut here is to simply search for the topic on Amazon and look for other books about the subject. If you find at least five other books with 15 or more reviews each, then chances are there's an active buy/sell market about the topic.

It might seem counterintuitive to write a book about a topic that has already been covered by several authors.

However, that's actually a great sign because readers love to purchase different books about a particular area. People like to learn about different perspectives, and your writing style might work better for them.

When I was studying JAVA (the programming language) in college, I read six different how-to books because I wanted to learn different insights and examples about how to code. So it's never a zero-sum game.

To summarize, the sweet spot for choosing a topic is at the intersection of something you're interested in, something you have experience in, and something that has an existing market. That's enough to guarantee you a winning topic.

However, there is one final circle that isn't mandatory, but is highly recommend for someone writing a book on the side.

Circle 4: Job-Related (Optional)

The fourth circle is about ideas that are related to your current job. If you're writing a nonfiction book, choosing something that's related to your career is going to help you with advantages in marketing, branding, and promoting your book.

Here's an example that explains how.

Let's say you're a pediatrician and you've come up with two separate ideas for your book.

One is about "Children's Bedtime Stories," and the other is about "Avoiding trips to the Children's Emergency Room."

Both are good options because they meet the first three criteria (interest, experience, and market).

However, only the second topic meets the fourth criteria because it's related to your job as a doctor.

Choosing the second topic gives you several advantages.

First, you'll establish yourself as an authority figure in the medical space. If your book is successful, you'll be quoted as an expert in the media using bylines such as "Dr. Jane Smith, author of a bestselling book about child emergency room visits." This will give you more credibility in your field than if you were associated with a bedtime story book.

Second, your network can be used for leverage. Chances are that as a doctor, you have a lot of doctor friends. This means that they can help out with endorsements and testimonials. They can also help promote your book to their own patients because the book is inherently related to their field as well.

Finally, it gives you a boost in terms of selling consulting services or becoming a paid speaker. A published book about a related field is a powerful marketing tool that makes it easier for you to pursue those additional opportunities.

All those advantages are multiplying factors that you won't gain if you write about an unrelated topic such as a children's bedtime story book.

To reiterate, the first three circles would suffice to choose a successful topic, but including that fourth one would be better for you in the long run.

Step 2: Narrow It Down

The next step is to narrow down the topic of your book.

This is where you'll take the high-level ideas you came up with in Step 1 and turn them into concrete goals that you want to accomplish for your reader.

For example, if you selected "personal finance" as a general topic in Step 1, then this step is about refining it to something like: "My book will help employees working in the US and making less than $50,000 per year get out of debt."

So you're basically niching down your topic. This is important because you want to target a specific problem that can be covered in a short book.

You can accomplish that in one of two ways:

1) Narrow down the target audience

The target audience is the demographic that would be interested in your book. So narrowing down your target audience means that you're using a subset of the original broader audience by adding more traits or adjectives to it.

Here are a couple of examples:

Example 1
• [Broad Audience] "Women over 45."
• [Narrow Audience] "Women over 45 who are married and have two or more kids."

Example 2
• [Broad Audience] "College students."
• [Narrow Audience] "College students living in Germany who are pursuing a degree in engineering."

2) *Narrow down the outcome*

Similarly, narrowing down the outcome of your book is about adding more constraints to your original broad topic.

Example 1
• [General Outcome] "Learn how to cook."
• [Narrow Outcome] "Learn how to cook vegan meals for under $10 a recipe."

Example 2
• [General Outcome] "Lose fat."
• [Narrow Outcome] "Lose three inches of fat from your belly without dieting."

Narrowing down your topic will help you in several ways. First, you'll avoid spreading yourself too thin because you'll be focusing on a more defined area. Second, you'll save a lot time on writing because you'll be typing fewer words. And third, you'll give your readers what they want because most people enjoy quick, short reads anyway. So it's a win-win for everyone.

This exercise is more of an art than a science. You're basically doing a blend of typical market research and gut-checks.

The secret to doing this effectively is to research specific pain points for a certain demographic.

Most people buy nonfiction books to solve a problem. So if you can figure out *who* those people are and *what* problems they're trying to solve, then you'll find the narrow topic to pursue.

Here are a few ideas that will help you do that (listed in order of priority):

Tip #1: Look inward

Start by looking at your own knowledge and experience.

What were your main challenges when you first experienced the book's topic? What was most frustrating to you? What did you learn the hard way?

Those are challenges that other people would naturally have as well.

If you selected a topic that's job-related in Step 1 (i.e., the fourth circle), then you probably already know what those pain points are from your daily job. Think through the main questions you get as a practitioner and the services you're getting paid for.

I have a friend who's a child psychiatrist and is interested in writing a book about her field. However, writing a general book about child psychiatry is much too broad. So I asked her to tell me the most frequent reason patients visit her, and she said it was depression. I then asked what age range or gender those patients fell into, and she said that 80% of them were female and were between 14 and 17 years old. Those answers are a huge indicator of a winning narrow topic:

"A book that helps teenage girls deal with depression."

Tip #2: Read Amazon reviews

Another idea for finding pain points is to read Amazon reviews of similar books. This is a great strategy because you'll research viewpoints of readers who already paid for those books and took the time to review them. So those same people might end up being your customers, and you'll be honing in on what they need.

The key is to read both the positive *and* negative reviews of those books to find any potential patterns.

Positive reviews

From the positive reviews, you can learn about what people find helpful. Look for trigger phrases such as "The best thing about this book is..." or "What separates this book from others is..." for ideas you can niche down on.

For example, I just read a positive review about a "Dating for Men" book. The reviewer stated that he enjoyed learning about walking up to a woman without a script and just saying "Hi, I'm so and so, and I'd like to get to know you." He mentioned that this technique works better than memorizing corny lines that are typically advocated in generic dating books.

So from that review, I thought of an idea about another book topic: "How unconfident men can walk up to women and start a conversation without sounding like creeps."

I don't know if that would be a successful topic, but it's just one idea based on the analysis of a single review. If you read multiple positive reviews about several related books, then you'll get to see a pattern that will help you narrow down your topic.

Negative Reviews

Similarly, from the negative reviews, you can learn about what people were disappointed with. Look for trigger phrases such as "This book wasn't helpful for..." or "This book lacks..." to analyze what people don't want.

For example, I just read a negative review of a book about dog training. The reviewer stated that the information was too overwhelming for someone who's a complete novice, and that she was confused about what to do during her first few days after bringing a dog home. She also stated that her dog was a puppy and that the book seemed like it was geared toward full-grown dogs.

So one idea here is to write a book that helps inexperienced dog owners train their new puppy during the first seven days.

Again, this is just an idea, but you get the point.

If you want to save time in this step and avoid having to read hundreds of positive and negative reviews about each book, here's a little timesaver. Amazon lists the "Top positive review" and the "Top critical review" for each book. Those are the top two reviews that are voted by the public as the most helpful for prospective buyers. So if you read just those two reviews for each book, then you'll save yourself a lot of time and still glean a few good ideas from them.

Tip #3: Check Internet Forums

Another great idea to narrow down your topic is to

check out internet forums.

Forums, or message boards, are websites where people can hold online discussions about a particular topic.

Those can be a treasure of ideas to narrow down your topic because people usually post questions on them to get help.

To find forums related to your book, simply type the following in the Google search bar:

forum: Your topic

This is a special operator that returns only forum-type websites. Then, from the search results, copy one of the URLs, and type the following into Google again:

"How do I" site:URL

This will basically search for any question that has a "How do I" phrase within that forum.[3]

You'll then get a list of results about different discussions that you can target.

For example, I searched for the following on Google:

forum: massage

And came up with the following URLs about the topic of massage:

www.massageprofessionals.com/forum
massageplanet.net

---

[3] Credit for this technique goes to Pat Flynn and his awesome *Will it Fly?* book where this strategy is discussed in-depth.

thaihealingmassage.com/forum

I then copied the first one and typed the following in Google:

> *"How do I"*
> *site:www.massageprofessionals.com/forum*

The search results gave me a list of several discussion threads that had a "How do I" phrase in them. One of them was someone asking, "How do I find clients if I just graduated out of school?"

So I read through the answers and came up with the idea of a book to help recent massage therapy school graduates get their first ten paying clients.

You can also get creative and search forums by sorting topics based on the date of the comments (more recent is better) or number of comments, which are indicators of hot trends and popularity.

Tip #4: Do a survey

Finally, if you have the time, you can run a short survey by setting one up for free on SurveyMonkey or Google Forms, and send it to people who might be interested. Use Facebook, Twitter, LinkedIn, or other social media outlets to share it and get some responses.

The key to a good survey is to keep it really short (no one has time for a lengthy one) and to ask only three questions:

• *"What's your #1 challenge or frustration regarding <Topic>?"*
• *"What would be your ideal outcome when it comes to*

<Topic>?"
• *"What resource would be really helpful for you about <Topic>?"*

Then analyze the responses for repeat patterns and potential problem statements.

Keep in mind that you don't have to do all of the above exercises to narrow down your topic. They're listed in order of priority from most important to least important. So if you're really short on time, then just do the first one, "look inward." You won't be missing out if you skip out on the remaining ones.

Output of this step

The output of this step will be the following sentence:

"My book will help <Target audience> <Outcome>"

Simply fill in the blanks with your <Target Audience> and <Outcome>.

Here are a couple of examples that I used for my own books:

Example 1: My book will help <managers who lead remote teams> <learn how to influence their team members to get things done>.

Example 2: My book will help <employees who rely heavily on email to collaborate with their teams> <understand how to write better emails and improve their communication skills with their team members>.

You might end up with several statements, and that's ok. If you get a couple that are related, then don't be tempted to combine them into one book. It's better to keep them separate and publish one of them as another short book in the future.

Step 3: Choose a Title and Subtitle

The next step is to choose a title and subtitle for your book.

The objective here is to take the output from Step 2 and come up with an attractive title so that people will be interested in learning more about your book.

For example, if you listed the following output statement in Step 2:

"My book will help teenage girls deal with depression."

Then this step is about choosing a title and subtitle such as:

"Reversing Depression: A step-by-step plan for teenage girls who want to be happy again."

Title vs. subtitle

There are some minor differences between the title and subtitle of your book, but they serve the same purpose.

Your title is the first phrase that is listed on your book. It's your one-second description that appears in the largest font size on your book cover. The general recommendation is that your title should be between one and five words in length. That's because you want to make it easy to pronounce and memorable. You also want to make it simple for people to mention your book on social media and in interviews.

Your subtitle builds on and supports your title. It is

usually longer (four to fifteen words in length) and can include more descriptive words to expand on your topic. If your title is the one-second description, then your subtitle is your mini elevator-pitch. So they complement each other.

Choosing a title and subtitle will take a few cycles, so don't worry about nailing this exercise down on your first pass. You'll also have the chance to test and refine in the next few steps.

Here are some guidelines that will help you out.

Anatomy of a great title and subtitle

A great title and subtitle should ideally do four things: grab attention, explain the outcome, define the audience, and contain keywords.

You don't have to cover all four elements in both the title and the subtitle. A couple of those elements can be addressed by the title and the other two by the subtitle.

You can use your title to grab attention and contain keywords, and use the subtitle to explain the outcome and define the audience. The idea is to try your best to have all four of those elements covered between both.

1) Grab attention

The first thing a book title should do is grab the attention of your prospective reader. The goal is to make them stop what they're doing and click on your book to learn more. Your audience will be bombarded by hundreds of other book titles, and your book needs to stand out among the crowd.

You can do that by being relevant, controversial, sneaky, or funny. This will require a bit of creativity, so there are no hard and fast rules.

Also, keep in mind that your attention-grabbing element doesn't have to describe the entire topic of your book. You can choose an angle that covers only a portion of it.

For example, when I was thinking about a title for my own book about email, I considered the following phrase: "Email Communication for Teams."

Although this title accurately described the general topic of the book, it wasn't very attention-grabbing. In fact, it was boring. I had to think about a creative angle to stand out. So I thought about the number one pet peeve that people have about email in a corporate environment: the use of "reply all." And after a few iterations, I came up with *Don't Reply All* as the main title.

It was a hit because everyone hates "reply all" and it made people smile.

So although my book was not *only* about the topic of "reply all" (it was covered in just one chapter in the entire book), I went with an attention-grabbing element that wasn't necessarily descriptive.

Here are a few other examples of book titles that grab attention.

• *Example 1: Trust me, I'm lying: Confessions of a Media Manipulator*
• *Example 2: Hardcore Self Help: F**k Anxiety*
• *Example 3: Invisible Ink: A Practical Guide to Building Stories that Resonate*

2) Explain the outcome

The second thing your title should do is explain the outcome so that buyers know exactly what they're getting out of your book.

If you wrote a clear output statement in Step 2, then this part should be fairly straightforward.

You'll just be rephrasing the outcome so that it's more title-friendly.

The following phrases can help you accomplish that:

- "How to <outcome>"
- "A Step-by-Step plan that <outcome>"
- "X Tactics for <outcome>"
- "X Steps to <outcome>"
- "Learn how <outcome>"
- "X Easy Tips <outcome>"

For example, if your output in the previous step was:

"My book will help <mothers who have very little time> <create vegetarian recipes for their kids>"

Then this could be rephrased to the following title options:

- *Example 1: "How to make delicious vegetarian recipes for picky eaters"*
- *Example 2: "21 Easy Vegetarian Recipes for Finicky Kids"*

The goal is to explain the outcome so that your readers know what they're gaining after reading your book.

3) Define the audience

The third thing your title should do is define the audience.

Your prospective customers should know exactly who the book is written for.

If you did a good job with the output statement in the previous step, then this part is also simple.

You'll basically take the target audience and try to reference it in the title somewhere.

You don't have to *explicitly* state the target audience. You can just allude to it.

For example, here's a title of a successful book by Marty Neumeier:

"ZAG: The #1 Strategy of High-Performance Brands"

The book targets marketers and business leaders who want to create a strong brand for their service or product, but the title doesn't explicitly state that. All it does is hint at the fact that the target audience is interested in developing a high performing brand. And that's totally fine.

The point is that if someone reads the title, they should be able to determine if the book applies to them.

4) Contain relevant keywords

Finally, your title should contain some relevant

keywords in it.

Keywords are the words or short phrases for which people search on Google or Amazon that relate to your book's topic. If you use relevant keywords in your title, your book will appear higher in organic searches, which will translate into more people seeing your book (i.e., more sales).

To find what those relevant keywords are, you need to do what's called "keyword research," and here are some thoughts about it:

First, keyword research is a topic that can take up several books, so we won't be able to get into a lot of detail here. There are also many tools and websites that help you do detailed research about your topic. Simply Google "How do I do keyword research" and you'll get a ton of free resources to read. You can also check out the free *Keyword Planner* tool (for Google Keyword Research) or *Merchant Words* (for Amazon keyword research).

Second, I think keyword research is actually over-hyped. To be honest, I don't think it's particularly necessary, so I don't give it that much attention. You can actually skip keyword research entirely, especially if you've done everything else up to this point.

Finally, the main value of keyword research is that you'll use words familiar to a wider audience. So to me, keyword research helps with alternate word selection within a specific industry. For example, when I was doing keyword research for my *Influencing Virtual Teams* book, I could have used different word phrases for "virtual teams" such as "remote teams" or "telecommuting teams." But "virtual teams" was used a lot more frequently in terms of search volume on Amazon and Google, so I stuck with it to gain more from an organic search perspective.

Again, don't worry too much about keyword research. If you're quite familiar with the industry you're writing about, and already know what keywords or jargon everyone uses, then you're good to go.

Output of this step

The output of this step will be several title and subtitle combinations for your book.

Pick the top two or three combinations that are the best at grabbing attention, defining the outcome, explaining the audience, and containing relevant keywords.

The next step is about testing which title works best and iterating on it a few times to refine it.

Step 4: Test and Iterate

In this step, you'll take the best two or three titles from Step 3 and test them out with your prospective readers.

From the feedback you get, you might refine your topic or audience, and possibly recalibrate your title.

The goal is to come up with the final title and subtitle that you'll settle on for your book.

Here are a few ways to test your title options.

1) Ask your friends and colleagues

The simplest and fastest way to get feedback is from people you know. Ask friends, family members, and colleagues what they think about the titles. Give them the options and ask them to give you their honest opinion.

Explain that you haven't started writing the book but that you want to know if you're on the right track.

Facebook is a great medium for that. Here's a sample status update you can post:

> *"Friends - I'm writing a book about <Topic> and would love your thoughts on which title works better.*
>
> *<Title A>*
>
> *Or*

<Title B>

If you also have any suggestions for improvement, please feel free to share!"

2) Ask a stranger

Another great idea is to ask a complete stranger what they think about your title options. This might feel a bit uncomfortable, but the feedback you will get is invaluable because strangers are usually very honest. They won't worry so much about hurting your feelings.

Whenever you're waiting in line at say a coffee shop, start a conversation with the person behind you by saying something like:

"Hi there - I know this might seem like an odd question, but I'm a new author writing a book about <Topic> and I'm gathering some feedback about what random people think about it.

"I have two titles in mind. One is <Title A> and the other is <Title B>.

Which do you think is the one that more people would be interested in?"

Then start a casual conversation by asking why they think one is better and whether you can make any improvements.

3) Run a survey

Finally, you can also run a survey to get feedback on your title options. This is similar to what you did in Step

2 to narrow down your topic, but the questions will focus on which title is best and how you can make it better.

Use SurveyMonkey or Google Forms as free options to email people and ask for feedback.

Feedback results

From all the feedback results you get, start looking for patterns among the responses. A few people might be super-enthusiastic about one title, making it a clear winner, while others might have clarifying questions about another, meaning it will need some refinement.

The objective is to gain validation on your options and iterate on them. If people are not clear or not interested about a title now, then they won't be clear or interested about it later. So you might as well revisit the title while it's still early on and you haven't invested a lot of time or energy in creating the book.

Summary of the first four steps

The first four steps that we just covered are the most important in this entire process. They constitute the first half of the battle that will make or break your book. The remaining steps are all about grunt work (outlining, writing, editing, etc.), which are obviously crucial, but your success in those remaining steps will depend on how well you nail down the first four. So make sure you follow them carefully.

Here's a quick recap of those four steps:

Step 1 was about choosing a general topic for your book

by listing ideas in four circles: Interest, Experience, Market, and Job-Related (optional, but recommended). The ideas that fall under the first three circles, and preferably all four, are the topics you should focus on.

In Step 2, you take the general topics you came up with in Step 1 and niche them down by narrowing the audience and/or the outcome. You can accomplish that by looking at your own experiences, reading positive and negative reviews of similar books on Amazon, checking internet forums, and running surveys. The goal of this step is to write an output statement such as "My book will help <Target audience> <Outcome>" so that you define the topic of your short book.

In Step 3, you take that output statement from Step 2 and use it to create a few title and subtitle options for your book. The title should be around one to five words in length so that it's memorable and easy to pronounce. The subtitle can be longer (four to fifteen words) and builds on your title. A good title and subtitle combination does four things: grabs attention, explains the outcome, defines the audience, and contains relevant keywords.

In Step 4, you take the best two or three title and subtitle combinations from Step 3 and test them with people to get feedback. You can do that by asking friends, colleagues, or even strangers. You can also run surveys. From the feedback, you'll then analyze the responses for common patterns to refine your title and subtitle. You then keep iterating on Steps 2, 3 and 4 until you are comfortable with the final choice.

Once you've settled on a title and subtitle, you'll move on to the next step, which is about outlining your book.

Step 5: Outline Your Book

In this step, you'll be outlining the content of your book by documenting the different section and chapter headings.

I like to keep things really simple here by dividing the outline into three main parts.

Part 1 is the introduction, Part 2 is the main body, and Part 3 is the conclusion.

For a short book, you don't really need to get any fancier than that.

Here's what goes into each part.

Part 1: Introduction

The introduction should cover a few basic things.

First, it should lure the reader to continue reading. The biggest turn off for readers is a dry and boring intro. To create an intriguing introduction, start by directly addressing the problem that your book is trying to solve. Stories work really well here, but keep them short and make sure you tie them back to the top challenges that your readers face.

Second, your introduction should explain who you are and why people should listen to you (keep this brief as well). This is important because readers want to know what makes you qualified to write the book. As I stated earlier, you don't have to be an expert in the topic of your book, but you have to show that you know what you're talking about.

Third, your introduction should explain why your book is unique and why people should read it. You have to reinforce the outcome and the target audience so that your readers feel comfortable that they're in the right place. Don't be shy about repeating some content that was already listed in your book description or title. It keeps your message on point.

Here are a few other tips about writing a good introduction:

- Reference statistics if you need to, but don't overdo it.
- Use headings and subheadings to break up lengthy paragraphs.
- Be enthusiastic and positive—you want your readers to be energized about reading.
- Keep it simple—you don't have to promote a flashy dog & pony show.

Part 2: Main body

The main body contains the meat of your content. It's the reason why people want to read your book.

This section includes the substance of your topic, and solves your readers' problems.

If you had used a "Step-by-step" or "X Tactics" phrase in your title or subtitle, then list out each of those steps or tactics as part of your outline.

For example, if you're writing a book entitled: *"Golf for Beginners: 25 tactics to improve your golf drive in a weekend,"* then your tactics would be:

Tactic #1: Hold your golf club properly.
Tactic #2: Stand using the "shoulder-width"
technique.
Tactic #3: Relax your waist for the pull.
Etc...

The idea is to outline what's going to go into each chapter of your book.

Similarly, if you're organizing your book by theme instead of tactics or steps, then list what those themes are as headings in this part.

You can use some of the research you did earlier (when reading Amazon reviews or conducting surveys) to come up with powerful chapter titles here. For example, if you're writing a travel book about visiting Tokyo and you read a negative review about a Tokyo travel guide that didn't include the must-see places in the city, then you can turn that into one of your headings.

"The top five must-see places in Tokyo if you're short on time."

You get the point.

The one thing you should be cautious about is that the outline of your main body should always deliver on the title and subtitle of your book. As you draft out the chapters, do a continuous self-check to make sure you're still in line with the main objective of your book. Otherwise, you might drift off topic.

Part 3: Conclusion

The conclusion should be a short chapter that summarizes the content of your book.

In this section, you reinforce the outcome again by stating something like "We just covered <Outcome> that will help you <Benefit> as a <Target audience>"

For example,

"We just covered 55 easy green smoothie recipes that will help you save time as a busy mother of little kids."

Then go over the main concepts to remind your readers of the important takeaways.

Keep the conclusion brief and tight. You want to just wrap things up and close the loop on your book.

At the end of your conclusion, you can leave your email address or website for readers to contact you with any questions. You can also politely ask your readers to leave you an honest review on Amazon.

Output of this step

The output of this step is a page or two that includes your book's outline. Label the three main parts of your outline "introduction," "main body," and "conclusion." Then include chapter headings and subheadings underneath each part. You can also jot down notes in your outline to remind yourself what you want to write about.

You are now ready for the best part: writing your book!

Step 6: Write Your Book

In this step, you'll write your book.

This is probably the longest and hardest part in the entire process, and you'll spend the majority of your time in it. Writing can feel like an endless and lonely journey, but when you're done you'll know it was worth it.

The primary reason why people never finish their book is that they don't have the time for it. The second reason is that it's hard work.

As a person who works full time, I get both those reasons. I understand how work, life, and stress always get in the way of finding the time. I also know how mentally taxing writing can be. It takes a significant amount of effort to think about things like word choice, structure, content, flow, and style.

However, I'm living proof that you can write your book even if you don't have the time for it.

Here are thirteen tips, strategies, and mental shifts that will help you out.

Tip #1: Force a block of time

Let's start with the most important writing tip that you can learn.

There is absolutely no way you can write your book if you don't set aside some time for it. There are no secrets or magic pills about writing. It's all about forcing a block of time and creating a habit around it.

My recommendation is to dedicate 30 minutes a day, five days a week to write your book.

That's because anyone can find 30 minutes a day—even over-worked, full-time parents. You can wake up a little bit early or go to bed a little bit late. Or have a shortened lunch. You could even split the 30 minutes a day up by writing 15 minutes in the morning and 15 minutes at night if you have to.

Writing five days a week instead of seven means that you can take the weekends off. So that will help you manage your time a little bit better, and give you a mental break so that you stay motivated when you get back into it.

Tip #2: Don't write just once a week

Thirty minutes a day, five times a week equates to 2.5 hours a week. So you might ask if it makes sense to block 2.5 hours on a Saturday morning and write just once per week. I strongly recommend against that.

Going a full week without writing will make you lose momentum and you'll eventually give up.

The idea behind writing five days a week is to keep your creative juices going. Whether consciously or subconsciously, throughout the day your mind is going to be thinking about your book, and that's an important part of the process. You can only trigger that thought process if you give your brain a push by writing every day throughout the week.

Also, understand that thirty minutes is a *minimum* guideline. If you feel one day that you're on fire and can go on for much longer than that, then certainly don't stop. Those are rare bursts of creativity that you should take advantage of.

Tip #3: Find your quiet zone

A quiet zone is a physical or mental space that you use when you're writing. This is a zone that should be distraction-free. Find a spot where you can silence your phone, switch off the TV, shut down Facebook, and ask your family members not to interrupt.

I work from home, which means I write my books in the same home office that I work from. This makes it harder for me to shift my mode from working to writing. So when I'm in writing mode, I trick my brain by modifying my environment. I turn my space into a quiet zone by turning off all the lights in my room and closing the shades so that the only light source comes from my computer monitor. I then use ear plugs and put on some faint classical music in the background to drown out any ambient noise. This helps me focus only on writing and nothing else.

Tip #4: Forget fancy tools

You don't need any fancy tools to write your book. Microsoft Word or something similar like Google Docs or Apple Pages is all you need. For organizing your ideas, you can use regular post-it notes or index cards.

When you start out, you'll be tempted to use the latest sexy tools that other authors use. While some of those tools do have cool features, you'll be wasting time on learning them instead of concentrating on what matters: writing your book.

Having said that, one awesome tool I started using *after* I wrote my first book is Scrivener. It helps me organize my ideas and chapters in a much easier way. I can also view a "bird's eye" perspective of my book chapters in the margin which gives me satisfying feeling of control. But Scrivener takes a bit of time to learn and get used to, so I would stick to a basic word processor like MS Word when starting out.

Tip #5: Shoot for 10,000 to 12,000 words

The biggest time saver when writing your book is to write fewer words. As I mentioned earlier, people don't like long reads. They want short books that solve their problem quickly. A sweet spot is 10,000 to 12,000 words, which is around 60 to 70 pages of a printed book.

Of course, this target word count is just a guideline. So don't get hung up on the exact word count if you need to write a couple of thousand words beyond that range.

Tip #6: Avoid setting a daily word count

Some authors recommend forcing a "word count" every day instead of time. Meaning that they recommend writing 500 to 1,000 words every day instead of dedicating thirty minutes a day. That didn't work so much for me because of two reasons.

First, I got very anxious every time I didn't meet the word count goal. So I started artificially pumping out words just to make it to 500 or 1,000. Second, as someone who has a full-time job, a family, and other obligations, I just didn't have the energy to write every day. I wanted to spend some of that time brainstorming, editing, and researching the topic.

So I found out that forcing a block of time works better for me.

At the end of the day, you have to set some form of metric to measure yourself against. Mine was 30 minutes a day, five days a week. Start with that and modify it if it doesn't work for you.

Tip #7: Don't set a deadline

Other authors recommend setting a self-imposed deadline for publishing your book as well (e.g., launch by December 7). The idea is that this will encourage you to write and stop procrastinating. But I think that's unnecessary if you follow the writing schedule of 30 minutes a day for five days a week. You'll eventually get the book written, and deadlines only add an unwelcome stress.

It should take you around six months or so to finish your book. But it might be a bit more than that if you're a slow writer or take your time with things like research. Authors who advocate shipping as fast as possible will disagree with me on this, but my philosophy is that publication dates don't matter. If it takes you a year or more to finish your book, then so be it. The point is to create something you're proud of and provides value for your readers.

Tip #8: Write in a casual tone

As you write your book, keep in mind that you're communicating with other human beings who prefer casual tones.

Many first-time authors think that they have to be formal or academic in their writing. But that's not what readers enjoy. They actually like simple sentence structures that are conversational and easy to digest.

Writing in a casual tone will also help you write faster because you'll be writing "as you speak" and not wasting time on fancy sentences.

Tip #9: Separate writing mode from editing mode

This has been one of the best pieces of advice that I've received about writing. I used to waste half an hour writing three sentences and then editing them over and over until I was satisfied.

But that strategy was so demotivating because I could never get a lot accomplished. I learned later that the best authors never edit while they type. They separate their writing mode from their editing mode.

So what I started doing was spend 30 minutes on a day doing nothing but pure writing. I threw down ideas on the screen by vomiting thoughts on my keyboard. I didn't care about grammar, spelling, or content mistakes. If I wrote something down that sounded like garbage, I didn't stop to clean it up. I just kept going.

The next day, I spent my 30 minutes looking over my

draft and editing, rephrasing and moving things around. I deleted sentences that made no sense and cleaned things up.

Separating writing from editing made my life a little easier, and I got much more accomplished in less time.

The key thing to remember is that the first draft of anything is going to be horrible, and that no one is ever going to read it. So give yourself permission to be imperfect.

Tip #10: Jot down notes anywhere, anytime

Another great time saver is to jot down ideas whenever and wherever they pop up. Throughout your day, you'll have some bursts of ideas about your book that you'll want to capture, and it's important to write those down as soon as possible before you forget them.

Here's what I do: After I write my outline (in Step 5), I keep a copy of it on my iPhone. Whenever I have some free time through my day (waiting for a friend at lunch or in line at the store), I look through it and start filling in the blanks on that outline.

This exercise is more about idea generation than actual writing. So I keep my notes brief and only jot down words that remind me of what I need to write about later. During my next 30-minute writing session, I take all those notes and start plopping them into my draft in the right places.

Tip #11: Don't fight writer's block

You will almost certainly get writer's block—that

dreaded state when you're completely stuck and not able to continue writing. The first thing you should realize is that everyone gets it. So you're not alone.

The second thing is that you shouldn't fight it, but rather work with it. In other words, when you're unable to proceed or think about writing, then do something else. Conduct more research, revisit your outline, or edit your previous work.

It's totally ok to take a temporary break from writing as long as you keep the momentum going.

Tip #12: Record your voice

Another tactic that helps writer's block (or writing in general if you find that too cumbersome) is to record your voice as you discuss the topic. You can then transcribe the recording as you re-listen to it afterward.

This makes a great first draft for your book that you can edit later on.

Here's how you do it.

Grab a good voice recorder (or use the free one built into your computer), and while looking at your outline, start talking about any one of the sections listed. Imagine someone interviewing you about a specific chapter and asking follow-up questions. If you stumble, keep going. Don't worry about pausing the recording to rephrase what you want to say. You can clean up all of that later.

Then, a day or so later, listen back to your recording and transcribe everything word for word. The familiar advice applies here: Don't edit as you transcribe because you'll mess up capturing your native thought process. After you're done, you'll end up with your first draft and can go back to re-read and edit your work.

Tip #13: *Hire a ghostwriter (optional)*

Finally, if you *really* don't want to write your book, you can outsource it by hiring a ghostwriter to write it for you.

This of course is the ultimate time saver.

However, I personally don't recommend it because of a few disadvantages.

First, the book will not feel like yours. When I wrote my first-ever book in 2006 (about information security), I hired a ghostwriter to do it for me. However, three chapters later, I asked him to stop because I felt that his writing style was not reflective of my own voice or brand. So I changed the structure of our arrangement where he turned into more of an editor than a ghostwriter and I ended up writing the book myself.

Second, it can get very expensive if you want to hire a qualified writer. Good ghostwriters can cost you thousands of dollars to write a high quality book.

Third, you are still going to have to do a bit of writing. At a minimum, you'll have to draft the full structure of your book. You will also need to guide your ghostwriter on content and research if he or she is unfamiliar with the book's topic. Plus, you will have to review their work constantly and give feedback on sentence structure and approach.

For those reasons, I encourage you to actually write the

book yourself. But if you still want to consider hiring a ghostwriter, you can find one on sites such as Upwork.com or Outsource.com.

Quick recap

We just covered thirteen tips to help you write your book on the side. A few of those are based on my own experience while others are based on the collective wisdom of authors who are much smarter than me. Keep in mind that what works for one person might not work for you. So try what you think works and modify accordingly.

The only tip that I think you *must* follow is Tip #1: Force a Block of Time. That's because it's nearly impossible to write your book if you don't establish a writing habit.

Step 7: Edit Your Book

The next step is to edit your book.

You can do this for free by asking your friends and family members to review the book for you, but I suggest you hire a professional editor instead.

That's because an editor who does this for a living will help you create a much better version of your book. They will give you an objective view for improving your manuscript.

The price of an edit job will depend on a few factors, including the length of your book, the extent of editing needed, and the experience of the editor.

But as a guideline, expect to pay anywhere between $200 and $600 to edit a 10,000-word book.

Side note: You can get quite finicky here and start looking at different types of editors ranging from proofreaders (the least expensive editors who look at only grammar and spelling errors) to content editors (the most expensive editors who look at everything including your paragraph structure and content), but you don't need to get that picky. A general editor would do.

To find one, you can use a free site such as Upwork.com where you can list your project (i.e., the job you'd like to get done) by including details such as your book's topic, title, word count, and any additional information. You'll then start getting bids by different editors who are interested in taking on your project.

You can check out each editor's previous work, and ask

them questions before hiring them. You can even negotiate the price if you feel it's too high.

At the end of the bidding process, you assign your project to a single editor and start working exclusively with them.

One thing to watch out for is to ask for at least a couple of rounds of editing. You're almost certainly not going to be satisfied with your edit after only one round. A professional editor should make at least two passes on your work to allow for some back and forth discussion.

After the editing is done, you'll have a finished manuscript that is ready for the next step. What I like to do at this point is share the manuscript with select readers who might be interested in endorsing the book. I reach out to colleagues and thought leaders who work in the same domain of the book's topic, and politely ask them if they're willing to provide a testimonial. This helps me in my marketing efforts later on when I launch the book.

Step 8: Format Your Book

The next step is to format your book so that it's ready for publication on Amazon.

What you'll be doing here is modifying your Microsoft Word file so that things like your font type, page breaks, heading styles, and table of contents are all formatted properly and appear exactly like you want them to in the ebook version.

The output of this step is a final Microsoft Word file that's edited and formatted according Amazon's requirements.

Amazon has a simple formatting guide (you can read it by visiting the *kdp.amazon.com* site) so you can format your book yourself if you're already familiar with Microsoft Word's features.

The great thing about Amazon is that they provide you with an online previewer that helps you preview how your book's text will look like on different devices. Using your computer's browser, you can select a Phone, Tablet, or Kindle E-reader, and check how the formatting and fonts show up in those devices through a test window.

If you don't have the patience or skills to do the formatting yourself, then you can hire someone to do this task on Upwork.com as well.

As a side note, most editors are actually trained on formatting as well, so what I do is hire an editor who also formats the book for me by paying them a little extra. It usually costs no more than an additional $50 for formatting my book.

Step 9: Design a Cover

This step is about designing a cover for your book.

The output of this step is a single image file (JPG or TIFF format) that will be uploaded to Amazon and used as the cover image of your book. The specifications of how large the image file should be and what pixel ratio you should use are all published on Amazon's KDP site (*kdp.amazon.com*).

If you're not a designer yourself, then you have three options to create your book cover:

Option 1: Design it for free
Option 2: Design it for cheap
Option 3: Design it professionally

My recommendation is to always do it professionally (option 3), but let's discuss each option first.

Option 1: Design it for free

You can create a cover for free by using Amazon's built-in cover creator. This is a very simple process where you can choose a book cover design from several templates. All you do is pick one that you like, change the colors, and then type the title, subtitle, and author name. You hit "save" and voilà, you get a cover you can use for your book. The whole thing takes 60 seconds.

Option 2: Design it for cheap

The second option is to create a cover by hiring an

inexpensive designer. Simply visit Fiverr.com, type "Book Cover Designers" in the search bar, and pick a designer who will design the book cover for you for only $5.

Option 3: Design it professionally

The third option is to hire a professional graphic designer to design the cover for you. This can cost you anywhere from $100 to $500 (or even more). I've spent around $300 to design each of my own book covers.

While it might be a bit pricey, my recommendation is to always hire a professional designer.

That's because a well-designed cover is your only chance at a solid first impression. If you use Amazon's free option, or hire a very inexpensive designer on Fiverr, potential buyers are going to see it in the results.

Given that customers make split decisions when they're browsing online, they might skip over your book in response to its lackluster cover.

I know because I'm one of those folks.

I don't care if a book has over fifty positive reviews. If the cover looks like it was put together using Microsoft Paint, I'm going to assume that the content might be subpar at best. I realize I might be unfairly judging that book, but it's just how I make quick decisions, and I'm sure a few other people think the same way.

Moreover, designing a nice looking cover will also help you market the book to other sites later on. For example, blogs or news websites that might feature your book will have a higher chance of accepting it when they see a serious professional-looking cover as opposed to a cheap one.

How to design your cover professionally

You can design your cover professionally by either crowdsourcing it or by hiring a single designer.

Crowdsourcing is a method where you submit your design request through a site like 99Designs.com to a large group of designers. The designers then compete by submitting sample designs and you get to pick a winner.

On the other hand, hiring a single freelancer is basically working exclusively with one graphic designer from the start by finding them on a site like Upwork.com. You then work with them one-on-one on creating the design.

I've used both approaches and they're equally great.

Whichever method you use, you will need to make sure you write a good description for your book cover so that you avoid any potential headaches.

Here are a few tips that will help you:

1) Be very specific

Explain exactly what you want in the cover right upfront so that your designers can work with the guidance you provide them.

For example, if you want to include certain colors, or a specific font type, then state that in the description. A good idea is to share some cover designs of books that you like and ask them to create something similar.

You should also give them all the text that you want to have appear on the cover, including the title, subtitle, and author name.

2) Ask for different file formats

Explain to your designers that the book is going to be published as an ebook for Kindle. This will ensure they design a cover that meets the specifications required by Amazon. I usually include the link to Amazon's book cover design guidelines so they have it handy.

In addition to the main Amazon cover, I also ask for two more file formats. The first is a 3D version of the book cover so that I can use that image in my marketing. And the second is a generic format used for most other ebook covers including iBooks and Nook, which is slightly different that the recommended ratio for Kindle books. (You'll use this cover format in the future only if you ever break your KDP Select agreement, but it's good to have that file with you before your designer disappears.)

Those additional formats usually take the designer very little effort to create and should not increase the price they quote you. However, if you don't explicitly ask for them upfront, you'll probably get charged for them if you request them later.

3) Make sure it looks good at a width of 90 pixels

I like the title of the ebook to be readable when the cover is resized down to 90 pixels in width. That's because 90 pixels is the size of the thumbnails that readers see when they browse around in the Amazon marketplace, and that will help you from a visibility perspective. So I make sure I write that down in the description to the designer.

As you go through the design process, you'll undoubtedly get a few cover design options that you like and want to expand upon. Keep refining the designs until you settle on only two that you really like.

After that, I like to ask friends and family to pitch in by giving me their honest opinion about which they like more. A short status update on Facebook asking "Which cover do you like more? A or B?" works best.

If the votes are nearly equal, then I pick the one that I personally like more. But if the difference in votes is quite significant, then I pick the one that most people chose. The wisdom of the crowd counts for a lot here, and you have to trust what people think of your cover. So don't second-guess it.

The next step after designing a professional cover is to upload your finished Kindle book manuscript and cover file to the Amazon KDP portal to make it ready for publication.

Step 10: Publish Your Book

The next and final step is to self-publish your book on Amazon.

This is a step that intimidates many authors. However, it's a fairly straightforward process that should take no longer than 20 minutes. At most, it could take up to an hour if you're going to read everything in detail.

The process is also free. You are not charged anything upfront because Amazon takes a cut only after someone buys your book.

As you go through this chapter, keep in mind that Amazon updates its process every once in a while, so by the time you read this, they might have already changed a question or two. Don't be confused if what you get asked isn't covered here. Simply answer the questions and you'll be set.

To begin, you need two things to publish your book. The first is your completed and formatted manuscript (from Step 8), and the second is your book cover (from Step 9).

Next, visit the main Amazon Kindle Direct Publishing site on *kdp.amazon.com* to start the publishing process. This site is going to be your one-stop-shop for everything related to the self-publishing process. Sign in using your Amazon account (or sign up for one if you don't have one), click on "Create a New Title: Kindle eBook," then start filling in the information.

Here's a step-by-step guide to help you out.

Enter Your Book Details: The first few questions are

about your book's language, title, subtitle, author name, and series details. I leave the series, edition number, and contributors sections empty.

Then next section is the description for your book. This is what appears on the book's detail page on Amazon for prospective buyers to read before they purchase it. So spend some time on crafting a good description because this is like a sales page for your book. Address the problem you're trying to solve and how the book helps your customers. You can leverage parts of your introduction, output statement, and target audience to create a well-written description.

Publishing Rights: The publishing rights are about whether your book is a public domain work or you own the copyright. Because I own the copyrights to my books, I select the latter.

Keywords: Enter up to seven search keywords that are related to your book's topic. Keywords are words that will help readers find your book if they search for those particular words in the Amazon search bar. If you did any keyword research in the earlier steps, then you can use some of those words here. Otherwise, just use your best judgment.

Categories: Choose up to two browse categories for your book. This will make your book appear in the section of Amazon where buyers can find it by clicking through the different categories.

Age and Grade Range: If you're writing a book for children, or for a specific US grade school range, you can select a minimum and a maximum number for both here.

Publishing Option: Select "I am ready to release my

book now" or "Make my Kindle eBook available for Pre-order." The latter option allows your readers to buy the book up to 90 days in advance before it is published. The main advantage of this is that you can start promoting your book ahead of time. I tried this strategy once but it didn't really help that much, so I would just stick to the "I am ready to release my book now" option.

Manuscript: Here is where you upload your completed manuscript (from Step 8). You can also choose to enable Digital Rights Management (DRM), which protects your book from unauthorized distribution, and I recommend you opt in for that.

Side note: You can always go back and update your manuscript after you publish your book. That's the beauty of publishing an ebook on Amazon. So if you ever notice a typo a few months later, or you'd like to add a new chapter in the future, you can easily do so.

Kindle eBook Cover: This is where you either "Upload a cover that you already have" or "Use Cover Creator to make your book cover." The cover creator option is what you'll use if you decided not to have someone to design a cover for you in Step 9. It's a very simple to use tool and quite self-explanatory.

Kindle eBook Preview: After you upload your manuscript and cover, you can preview how your book would appear on different devices. You can keep making changes to your manuscript and re-check them using the online previewer until you are happy with the final result.

Kindle eBook ISBN: You can leave the ISBN and Publisher name empty because you don't need either if you're publishing on Amazon KDP.

KDP Select Enrollment: This is about whether you want to enroll in KDP Select for 90 days. As I mentioned earlier, this is Amazon's exclusive deal that I highly recommend you sign up for, so make sure you check this box.

Territories: Here's where you select the territories where you hold distribution rights for your book. You can either choose "All territories (worldwide rights)" or "Individual territories." I select "All territories (worldwide rights)."

Royalty and Pricing: This is the fun part where you'll choose a royalty percentage for your book and set its price on Amazon.com (the main US-based site). The price of your book is dependent on the royalty plan you select, and you have two options: either a 35 percent or 70 percent royalty.

If you choose 35 percent royalty, then you can price your book anywhere between $0.99 and $200.00 (a wide range).

However, if you choose 70 percent royalty, then you'll then you'll have to price your book between $2.99 and $9.99 (a narrow range).

As you can probably tell, Amazon wants you to price your book between $2.99 and $9.99 by giving you a higher royalty. That's because based on their internal data analytics, that's the optimal range for book prices.

When I first publish, I select a 35 percent royalty, and price my books at $0.99—the cheapest possible price— so that I maximize the amount of downloads. A week or so after my publication date, I change the royalty plan to 70 percent, and price my book at $2.99.

You can change the price of your book at any time, so it's a good idea to start low and then increase as you tweak it.

After setting the price of your book on Amazon.com (the US site), you can also set it for all the other international marketplaces in their local currencies (e.g., Amazon.in, Amazon.co.uk, Amazon.fr, Amazon.it, etc.).

Amazon automatically calculates the best equivalent prices of foreign currencies, and I just keep those recommended price points, but you can change them if you want.

Matchbook: This is an optional program that gives your customers a cheaper version of your ebook if they purchase the paperback copy. You won't enroll in Matchbook at this point because you don't have a paperback version out yet.

Book Lending: Kindle Book Lending is also an optional program that allows your readers to lend your book to friends for fourteen days. I usually select this option because it maximizes exposure of my book through sharing.

If any of those questions confuse you, click on the "Help" buttons to get clarity.

After that, you click on "Publish Your Kindle eBook" and that's it!

Your book will show up in around 48 to 72 hours on the Amazon marketplace for sale—sometimes even much faster than that.

Congratulations! You just completed the ten basic steps

to writing and publishing your book on the side. Technically, you don't need to do anything else at this point, and you can move on to writing your second book.

However, if you do have some more time and energy to invest, then the next few steps will give you some additional gains for your book. Those steps are entirely optional, so don't feel like you have to implement any of them. I'll explain the benefits of each in the following chapters.

Step 11 [Optional]: Launch Your Book

The phrase "Launch your book" is a bit ambiguous. To some people, it's about the marketing activities you do on the day you publish your book. To others, it's a much more comprehensive strategy that includes an entire team of professionals working on marketing the book over a period of weeks before, during, and after the publication date.

To me, launching a book falls somewhere in the middle. It simply means marketing it to as many people as possible.

My main objective in a launch is to maximize exposure of the book and get Amazon to promote it for me. The strategy I follow is to publish the book for free and then slowly increase its price over time. This maximizes the number of downloads and word-of-mouth advertising, while creating a sense of urgency so people act early and download it before the price hike.

There are hundreds of books and courses about how to do a successful book launch, so you can get quite sophisticated in this step.

However, given my limited time and resources, I keep things simple by following a five-phase plan.

Phase 1: Pre-launch

Several weeks before the publication date, I market the book by spreading the word about it. I connect with influencers such as bloggers, podcasters, and journalists to give them a heads up about the book's topic. I let them know that I'm willing to provide them with guest post articles or interviews if they're interested.

During this time, I continue to gather testimonials from early readers of the book, and ask them to publish their blurbs as reviews on Amazon when the book is out.

Side note: Reviews are extremely important, and Amazon relies heavily on them as indicators of a successful book. Consequently, Amazon monitors the authenticity of reviews very carefully. They only want honest reviews, so never (ever) write a fake review or hire someone to do it for you. You'll eventually get caught and you'll probably be penalized for it.

I also research websites, Facebook pages, Twitter handles, and any other forums that accept submissions for free Kindle books, and submit any online webforms ahead of time.

Phase 2: Launch free for five days

On the publication day, I launch the book for free and keep it free for the first five days. Amazon lets you do that only if you enroll in KDP Select. I email friends, colleagues, bloggers, and everyone else I reached out to earlier to let them know that the book is out. I also post regular updates on Facebook, Twitter, LinkedIn, relevant forums, and other social media channels.

This helps me get a high number of downloads. I also ask readers to spread the word to their colleagues and leave an honest review of the book on Amazon. Although I don't make any money during those five days, I drive a lot of awareness about the book.

Phase 3: Set price at $0.99 for seven days

After the five-day free period, I list the book at the cheapest possible price ($0.99) for around a week. My main goal here is to ride the wave of marketing that my book got in the free period. Most people won't think twice about spending $0.99 on a book they're interested in, especially if it has already generated some buzz.

This phase is more important than the previous one because Amazon's algorithm cares more about actual sales than free downloads. If Amazon notices that a large number of people paid for the book in a short time period, then it will start promoting the book for you to its customers, which will result in even more purchases.

To further drive sales during this period, I continuously update Facebook, Twitter, email lists, and other outlets with announcements that my book is available for "$0.99 for only X more days."

Phase 4: Raise price to $2.99 (or higher)

After a week, I raise the price to $2.99. This is the lowest price at which I can set my book to get a 70 percent royalty (as a reminder, if I priced the book anything lower than $2.99, I would only get a 35 percent royalty).

I then keep it at $2.99 for at least a month to get some steady-state data, and then test different prices by increasing the price $1.00 at a time.

Phase 5: Offer promotions

With KDP select, you can offer promotions to your

readers every 90-day period. So after your initial free book promotion, you have the option to offer the book again for free (for another five days) after 90 days have passed. You can also offer what's called a "Kindle Countdown Deal," which is a program that lists your book at a discounted price with a countdown timer showing customers the time remaining at that price level.

Make sure you take advantage of all those offer promotions so that you keep the buzz going about your book months or even years after the publication date.

Step 12 [Optional]: Turn Your Book into an Amazon #1 Best Seller

This step is about how to turn your book into an Amazon #1 best seller.

This means that your book will be listed at the highest ranking spot in a specific category on Amazon.

Before I explain how to accomplish that, let me start by sharing a couple of secrets about what this really means.

First, getting listed as an Amazon #1 best seller is much easier than most people think. In fact, a short while ago, a marketer wanted to prove how easy it was to game the system. So he took a picture of his foot, created a two-page book about it, and published it for sale on Amazon. He then asked a couple of his friends to buy the book (at $0.99), and his book became a #1 Amazon best seller after only three sales. The total time he invested in the process was only five minutes, and the total money spent on the book was only three dollars. It was that simple.[4]

Second, becoming a #1 Amazon best seller doesn't really translate into sales in the long run. I know this for a fact because both my books achieved #1 best seller status and stayed in that spot for around a week. However, my sales today are only at around one to five books a day. So it's not going to help you that much.

---

[4] Read the original article on the *Observer* here: http://observer.com/2016/02/behind-the-scam-what-does-it-takes-to-be-a-bestselling-author-3-and-5-minutes/

I think the only real advantage of being a #1 Amazon best seller is as a credibility indicator. You'll be viewed by people as an expert, and you'll get a bit of a boost in marketing and promotions. I also believe there is a certain level of respect that you gain by being listed as a #1 best seller. However, even all of those benefits are overrated these days because people have become kind of immune to the label. Nevertheless, it definitely won't hurt to have a #1 Best Seller banner associated with your book.

How does your book become an Amazon #1 best seller?

The key to becoming an Amazon #1 best seller is to list your book in a low-competition category and get a high number of sales in a short period of time.

A low-competition category is one where the current #1 bestselling book has an *Amazon Best Sellers Rank* of 20,000 or more. The *Amazon Best Sellers Rank* is a number that's listed publicly on every book's page, and it indicates how well that book is selling on Amazon. The larger the rank number, the fewer the sales. So a book ranked at 9,000 is currently selling fewer copies than a book ranked at 700.

Although Amazon doesn't publish data on the correlation between rank and sales figures, a lot of authors have shared some of their own numbers online, so you can get a fairly good idea of how many sales per day a book sells at a specific ranking.

For example, a book that has an *Amazon Best Sellers Rank* of 20,000 sells around 15 copies a day. A book that has a rank of 50,000 sells around four copies a day. And one that has a rank of 100 (a really good rank) sells around 950 copies a day.

So your goal is to find a #1 bestselling book that has a rank of 20,000 or more (i.e. it sells only around 15 copies or fewer a day), in a certain category. Then, if you list your book in that category and sell 16 copies of your book on any given day, your book will technically take over that top spot and become the #1 best seller in that category.

That's the whole strategy.

Here's a guide that'll explain how you can accomplish all of that.

1) Research low-competition categories of #1 books

Start by browsing for books in the Kindle store that are related to your book's topic.

For example, if your book is about "Using microscopes for kids," then type that phrase in the Amazon search bar, and click on some of the books that pop up in the results.

On each book's page, scroll down to the *Product Details* section where you'll find two pieces of information.

The first is the *Amazon Best Sellers Rank* number, and the second is the ranking within the category of where that book is listed under.

For example, one of the books that popped up when I searched for "Using microscopes for kids" is:

"Pippa's Progress - First Adventures With a Microscope For Children"

When I clicked on that book, I scrolled down to the details section and noted that the *Amazon Best Sellers Rank* was showing up as #239,318.

Underneath that number, the rankings and categories that showed up included the following:

• *#4 in Kindle Store > Kindle eBooks > Nonfiction > Science > Experiments, Instruments & Measurement > Microscopes & Microscopy*

• *#1812 in Kindle Store > Kindle eBooks > Crafts, Hobbies & Home > Crafts & Hobbies*

This means that the book is listed in two categories, and it's ranked as #4 in one of them and #1812 in the other.

Each category and subcategory navigation trail is a hyperlink, so you can click on any of those breadcrumbs to research that specific category. Make sure you click on the last one in the navigation trail, because that's the category that the book is listed under.

For example, I clicked on the *"Microscopes & Microscopy"* link, which took me to a page that listed all the top 100 paid books in that category.

I then looked at the #1 ranking book, which had a title of:

"Lab Values: 137 Values You Must Know to Easily Pass the NCLEX!"

So I clicked on that book, scrolled down to the Product Details, and found out that the *Amazon Best Sellers Rank* shows up as #20,480.

That's a good sign because the book is ranked at around 20,000, which means it's only selling around 15 copies a day to achieve #1 best seller status. So if I list my book under the *"Microscopes & Microscopy"* category and sell more than 15 copies on a single day, then my book will become the #1 best seller in that category and I can claim that spot.

I realize this process is a bit confusing and that it'll take you a bit of time to do some digging around, but after a few tries, you'll get the hang of it.

2) List your book in that category

Recall in Step 10 (Publish Your Book) that you can list your book in two different categories. So you can find two low-competition categories to publish your book under and double your chances of becoming a #1 Amazon Best Seller.

During that step, you might not find the categories you want listed as part of the options. If that's the case, contact the support team and ask them to publish your book in the categories you want. It'll take them a day or two to respond, but they will make that change for you.

When you reach out, make sure you list the entire category navigation trail in your message, and not just the last subcategory, so that you don't confuse them:

Here's an example of a clear message:

"Hello, please list my book entitled <Your Book

Title> in the following two categories because they're not showing up in the listings:

Category 1: Kindle Store > Kindle eBooks > Nonfiction > Science > Experiments, Instruments & Measurement > Microscopes & Microscopy

Category 2: "Kindle Store > Kindle eBooks > Nonfiction > Science > Physics > Optics

Thank you"

3) Get a high number of sales

The last step is to plan on getting a high number of sales in a single day. Your best bet for this is on the day you change your book's price from free to $0.99. You can ask friends and colleagues who'd like to help you out to purchase the book on that day as well.

Although I technically need only 16 sales or more to hit the #1 best seller list, I like to plan on selling at least 20 to 25 copies on that day. This way, I have a nice buffer in case the estimates are a bit off.

If your book does hit the #1 list, Amazon will list an orange "#1 Best Seller" banner underneath it or right next to it. So make sure you take a screenshot if that happens, because it won't last forever!

Step 13 [Optional]: Gather Emails from Readers

This step about gathering emails from your readers so that you can stay in touch with them after they read your book.

Gathering email addresses from your readers will help you establish a relationship with them where you can send them follow up messages. You'll also build an audience to which you can sell future books, courses, or consulting services down the line.

If you've never collected email addresses using a blog or webform before, then the amount of time, effort, and money it'll take you to set this up could get overwhelming. You'll need to develop landing pages, craft emails, and set up auto-responders. Moreover, you'll need to create a high-quality "freebie" to bribe your readers to sign up, which might end up turning into another huge project.

That's why I list this step as optional for first-time authors. It's not worth learning all that before you publish your book. You can always do this step weeks or months later.

Here are the steps.

1) Create a freebie

A freebie is a free resource for your readers that persuades them to give you their email address in exchange for it. The resource should be a valuable and relevant piece of content that complements the information in your book. For example, it could be a template, a short reference guide, or even another book about the topic.

I highly recommend that you make this freebie as valuable as possible so that you impress your readers and have them trust that you're sending quality content.

You'll need a place to store your freebie, like a blog or a server, so that readers can download it after they sign up with their email address.

2) Set up an email marketing service account

An email marketing service provider is an online service that helps you collect email addresses and send follow-up emails to your subscribers.

You can use the service to create opt-in web forms, draft emails, and set up follow up auto-responders.

There are a ton of well-known email marketing service providers, but the one I've used for years is AWeber (*thecouchmanager.com/aweber*), which is free to use for the first 30 days.

3) Create a squeeze page

A squeeze page (or landing page) is a webpage that asks people for their email address so they can opt-in to receive the freebie.

There are many ways to create squeeze pages. You can create one yourself from scratch and host it on your blog. This is the cheapest way to do it, but it'll take some time to set up.

Or you can use a service like LeadPages (*thecouchmanager.com/leadpages*), which is a paid service, but super easy to use. I'm a big fan of them and still use them to this day.

A big benefit of using LeadPages is that you don't need to have a blog, and they even pre-fill some workable text for you that you can easily replace. LeadPages also links smoothly with AWeber on the backend so that the email addresses get updated when people opt-in. It takes me an average of two minutes to set up a squeeze page on LeadPages, so I highly recommend their service.

Disclaimer: I'm an affiliate for both AWeber and LeadPages. I've been using both those tools for years and can't live without them. In fact, if you already signed up to get the freebie for this book, then you just saw both those tools in action. The squeeze page was designed using LeadPages, and the email marketing service is provided by AWeber.

Visit the following page to download your free bonus if you didn't download it earlier (and see a real example of how LeadPages and AWeber work together):

http://www.thecouchmanager.com/wbsbonus

4) Update your book with the squeeze page link

After you set everything up and test the links out, you

need to go back and update your book with the link to your squeeze page. I usually include the link in a couple of places at least. The first is close to the beginning of the book, where I add a "Your Free Gift" chapter to explain the freebie and have a clear call to action. And the second place is closer to the end of the book as a reminder for those who missed it the first time.

Keep in mind that this update will mainly apply to new buyers of your book, and not the old ones. Although the latter group might be able to get it as well if they download the most recent version of your book, in most cases that doesn't happen, so you basically miss capturing the emails of those first few readers.

That's why it's better to do this step before you publish if you have the experience, time, and money for it. However, it's a process that could paralyze you and even keep you from publishing your book. So doing it later is totally fine.

Step 14 [Optional]: Expand Into Other Formats

The final optional step is to expand into other formats for your book, including a paperback version and an audiobook version. This will let you reach additional readers and give you some additional income streams because people like to consume information in different ways.

My recommendation is to start with the paperback version, because it's easier and cheaper to create than an audiobook version. You'll also make more sales with physical book copies that you would with audiobooks.

Here's a quick overview about how to create each version.

How to create a paperback version of your book

Creating a paperback version of your book from the ebook version is fairly straightforward, but it will require a little bit of modification.

CreateSpace is the company owned by Amazon that publishes "Print-on-Demand" books, which are printed at the moment people buy them so that you don't waste money on inventory. To create your paperback version, simply visit CreateSpace.com, click on "Start a title for free" and follow the instructions (this is going to be an exercise that's very similar to the "Step 10: Publish Your Book" process you followed earlier).

Here are a few tips that will help you out:

1) Clean your manuscript

Before you create your paperback, make sure your manuscript is print-friendly. This means there can be no live links. If your text has any link references in it, they obviously won't work in the physical version, so you will have to modify the text to spell out those URLs.

2) You'll need an ISBN

An ISBN (International Standard Book Number) will be required for your physical book. You can get one for free using a CreateSpace-assigned ISBN, or purchase a custom universal ISBN for $99. I usually go for the free option.

3) Choose trim size and interior type

You'll need to select the trim size, which consists of the physical dimensions of the book (I usually go with a 6" x 9" size), as well as the interior type (black & white or color), and paper color (white or cream).

All those will affect how many pages your book will be and the dimensions of your print cover and spine, so make sure you settle on all those options first before you create a physical cover design.

4) Upload your book file

When you upload your book file, you'll be able to see how your book looks like based on the trim size you selected. You'll also see any issues online using the Interior Reviewer tool. This will help you correct any interior issues early on.

5) Upload a print-ready cover

You'll need to hire a designer to modify your ebook cover design by amending it with a back cover and spine. The spine is the edge of the book that faces outward when a book is placed on a shelf. The width of the spine will depend on the number of pages of your book and the color of the paper (cream paper is slightly thicker than white paper). The requirements for this book cover are a little bit more complex, and you'll need to provide your designer with the information he or she needs to create a print-ready PDF cover for you.

6) Email support to link your two book versions

After you complete your setup and a paperback version is published, make sure you contact the CreateSpace support team to ask them to "link" the ebook and paperback versions on the Amazon marketplace. This way, both versions will show up on one page instead of on two separate ones.

How to create an audiobook version of your book

To create an audiobook version of your book, you'll need to record your voice while reading the book, and then upload the audio files to ACX.com.

ACX is the Amazon company that helps you turn your

book into an audiobook and facilitates the sale of your book through Audible, Amazon, and iTunes.

I'll keep this section short and state that I highly recommend that you hire a professional company to create an audiobook version for you. That's because if you do it alone, things like sound quality, accents, pacing, and background noises could all affect the quality of your audiobook. Unless you're experienced in this area, or have a premium studio setup, my suggestion is to have a professional narrator do this work for you.

While it may be a bit pricey, it will be money well spent to save yourself the headaches and most importantly the time. I had a friend who tried doing this on his own, but ended up spending more time on taping and editing the audio files than he did on writing the actual book.

There is one company I've used and highly recommend that does audiobook production. They're called Archangel Ink (*thecouchmanager.com/archangelink*) and have done a phenomenal job with my *Influencing Virtual Teams* project.

Conclusion

We just covered the entire process of writing and publishing your first nonfiction book while working a full-time job.

Here's a quick summary of the steps.

Steps 1 through 4 were about choosing a general topic for your book, narrowing it down, selecting a few title and subtitle options, and testing them until you settle on a final title and subtitle combination. Those first four steps are the most important in the process because they are the foundation for writing a book that matters.

Steps 5 through 8 were about outlining, writing, editing, and formatting your book. Those steps will take the longest time, but they're the most rewarding.

Step 9 was about creating a professional cover, and Step 10 was about publishing your book in 20 minutes on Amazon KDP.

Steps 11 through 14 were optional steps that you can pick and choose from if you have the time. They'll give you some cool advantages, but they're not necessary to get your book published.

Finally, always remember Rule #1: Write a really, really useful book.

It's a rule that keeps your readers front and center, and if you write a book that is worth their money and their time, you'll be successful as an author.

I hope you found this book helpful, and I wish you

success in your book-writing journey.

As Benjamin Franklin once said, "Either write something worth reading or do something worth writing."

I hope at this point you're highly motivated to do the former.

A Simple Request

Thanks again for reading this book.

I have one quick favor to ask.

If you enjoyed it, I'd be super grateful if you left an honest review about it on Amazon.

It'll take 60 seconds of your time and you don't have to use your real name if you're concerned about that.

But it'll mean the world to me because every single review counts.

Thanks so much for your kind support!

Cheers,

Hassan

Made in the USA
Middletown, DE
08 January 2019